The I of Me Now

The I of Me Now

Poems by
Jean Arnold

MAECENAS PRESS
1988

Library of Congress Cataloging in Publication Data
Arnold, Jean, 1921–
The I of me now: poems by Jean Arnold.

I. Title.
PS3551.R528I2 1988 811'.54–dc19 88-28236

ISBN 0-944266-00-2 cloth
ISBN 0-944266-01-0 paper

Printed in the United States of America

Acknowledgments

The author gratefully acknowledges permission to reprint seven poems that appeared in *The Texas Quarterly,* The University of Texas, Austin, some with revision and change of title. The italicized lines in "The Magazine," on page 67, are from a poem, "Jane Was with Me," written by Marvin Bell, published in *The Atlantic,* December 1982; he was most gracious in allowing them to be used.

The author would like to especially thank Mary Lynch Swander
for her continued help, criticism, and support.
Also, Mary Benefield Owensby for her generous sharing
of grammer and encouragement,
Beverly I. Allen for her unfailing interest,
and Marilyn Sue Fowler, who considered typing poetry
a normal part of her job as a physician's secretary.

To Norman Sage, my deepest appreciation for his integrity, expertise, and willingness to make it all fit.

Cover/jacket drawing: "July" by Rachel Matteson,
copyright 1984 by Rachel Matteson.

Book design and composition in Bembo at Annie Graham
Publishing Services, Iowa City, Iowa.

Printed by Thomson-Shore, Inc., Dexter, Michigan.
Distributor: Via, P.O. Box 704, Iowa City, Iowa 52244.

Contents

IV

for my parents, and Boots

"A great singer is he who sings our silences."
Kahlil Gibran, *Sand and Foam*

One

Mama's Towels

They are Springmaid, U.S.A.
Robust green with white petals
bursting from wisps of pink.
They remind me

of Mama's fishing hat
bumping down the bank as
she stepped wrong on the gravel,
and fell, twisted, like the tackle
in her box. A snapped ankle,
suddenly big. Her leg bigger
as a cast hardened over the pain.

The wide trail of the walker
as she stood. By the sink,
shaking a soapy rag under her arms,
wiping as more sweat came. I saw.
The swipe between legs for clean,
and the good child patting dry.
Her breath came hard. I turned
the wrong way. It should have been toward.

And later the embolus,
the dark shooting comet on target.
Her blood the enemy. I could not wipe it away
with the towels that lay folded, like Mama.

Before Morning

I remember the night
on the fourth floor,
when coma became
whatever coma becomes
when the breathing stops,
and I saw the brown and yellow
where the last needle was stuck.
The uncombed hair of sickness
lay still, and the dew of urine
was wiped away.

As I Drive By

I see the small ash
leafing above your stone.
If I could think of you
as twig size, and forget
the giant that twigs
become as they multiply
above the earth, then
it might be easier.

You come in snatches,
and wait for me beneath
the tree. Like roots,
your tapering fingers,
cracked by the cut
of winter, sink
into the ground,
holding you still.

The Feather Bed

It was always there from the time I came.
The white ticking billowed
when the feathers were beaten,
then settled into humps that moved
like blowing sand. In the spring and fall,

Mama tossed strong twigs from the orchard
into a scuttle scoured with lye soap. She added
a roll of cotton, baseball size, and a milkbottle
of kerosene marked with a big red X.

"Don't ever let the sun touch it," she'd say.
"It might catch fire." I lowered the shades
against the torch. We tugged the feather bed
onto the rug, and exposed the gaping springs.

Washing each spiral with soaked cotton,
we used the twigs like Q tips to scrub coils
difficult to reach. We killed bugs and eggs,
Mama said, but I never saw a one.

Somehow, the sweat and kerosene smelled clean.
After the chore, we ate cornbread with butter,
sitting on the bed. Then I'd remember, and run
to up the shades. Once I saw some hair stranded

over Mama's eye, and I saw her pull it back.
Her fingers were puckered, and one of them was cut.
I dove into the feather bed, crawling like a bug,
crawling and crawling, until I heard her laugh.

Gran

The two pictures hang together.

When photographed at six,
Gran sat on plush Victorian,
a young coquette

with loose curls
wispy on her forehead.
Her right ear was bared

and on her left fourth finger
there was a tiny diamond
cut to tease the light.

An off-shoulder dress
suggested flowing waltzes,
while her slim neck,
circled with ribbon,
was dressed for the dancing.

Gran was ten when her mother
gave birth, and died with fever.
Next oldest, she helped four others
toddle and wash, passing into a woman
while still playing with dolls.

At a picnic, she met John MacDuffy,
a railroad man from Fort Deposit.
He told her about planting pecan trees,
and making furniture in the barn,

and she told him about crocheting,
and the persimmon trees in her yard,
and about the kittens opening their eyes.

She was nineteen when they married,
and began their own family—
five children born into railroading.

They played engineer,
fireman, front brakeman,
rear brakeman, conductor.

They talked about 4-4-0's,
cupolas on cabooses,
wooden ties, metal spikes,
and T rails.

Always, they heard a train,
the Louisville-Nashville line,
each child born within sight
of a different depot.

That night in Montgomery,
when Mac was brought home
from an elder's meeting, sick,
Gran sat with him until dawn.

In early morning, she watched him go.

Determined to leave,
he walked the short distance
down Commerce Street
to the Union Station,

across rails and yard,
to the train shed
above the Alabama River
and its horseshoe curve.

She ran after him,
while wiping her floured hands
on a fresh apron, forgetting
the heaviness of her unborn.

There were two short bursts,
then a thunderous clunk of wheels
with metal screeching

as the engineer, with one thrust,
big-holed the train to a stop.
Then one long blast.

She stumbled down the track,
watched them pull Mac's body
from under the tender,

heard the confusion,
someone yelling,
"His foot slipped."

They could not stop her
from carrying his head
in her apron,
back down the rails,
to a waiting wagon.

As they took him away,
she stared at the ring
on her finger,
and bent to the ground,
crying out, only once.

When photographed at eighty,
Gran sat in a rocker
shared by generations
of cradled bodies
giving in to sleep.

Her eyes looked
beyond the camera,
beyond all of us.

A band of gold
rested in her lap,
its reflection often seen
as she waved to passing trains.

Shortcuts

The snow still haunted the ground
when I drove past and saw

the narrow brown, showing.
Angled toward the river

its lusty leg stretched long.
Toward the river and on,

to the big trees layered
with circles of years.

To the hole we dug
in Johnny Kraft's yard,

hoping to reach China.
To the Liberty store

and its barrel of sour pickles,
with a wooden fork floating inside.

I used that fork like a spear,
and jabbed the green whale.

And ran out the door,
onto the path, throwing,

with one big heave, the forked javelin
that never came down. Not ever.

Poor-Sam-Peabody
(A SPARROW'S SONG)

That day in the rain
when he flew to the top,
I aimed, as all children
in serious play. And shot.
The BB opened him with less
warning than a cat. He fell
close to the feeder filled
by me with the same hand
that pulled the metal kill.

In Passing
(GOLDFINCHES)

They came,
as though shot from the sun,
a flock, swarming into trees,

hundreds of them, singing
like musical dandelions
in the ravine.

In seconds, they were gone,
so quickly, I still saw
the leaves yellowed with wings.

September's Child

The sun is coming
out
onto my land
drying days of rain.

Its coming takes
from me
the quiet
that wetness gave.

Soft the rain cover
was,
overhead,
leaving

the pungent smell
of dampness
to draw me
into the earth.

October's Child

A little leaf
    fell to the ground,
        and, lying there,
            was never found.

The Wood Steps

Before the double-stick world,
there was a first time
I sat on the steps,
rolling bits of twine
to store in a kitchen drawer.

In a day of rain, as the sounds
striking themselves came
the steps were tumbling wet,
and lying on them, I turned
face up to catch whatever
the sky had to give.

On those steps, I held
the shadows of family
inside me, and ran up,
two at a time, stopping
as I saw the risers multiply
far beyond my breath.

Videos

I will want to hear their voices
after they die. Those drawls
rooted like mimosa and pine
in the clay of Alabama.

I can feel their r's
heal the jags in me,
while my own tongue
searches for its
lost language.

At ninety, Aunt Lele wheezes
into the phone. "You come, now,
you heah. Sweet child,
you heah me!"

My kin are going.
The tapes are not made.
I can still catch
their humped wrinkles
swinging on the porch,
see them stiffen
shyly on camera.

The trip must be made.
Their stick fingers
shake in my face.
Come on. Come on.

Two

A Boy from Curve

I

Speak to all other fathers, my father,
You who never spoke to your own.
Your thin boy feet, powdered brown

with Curve, Tennessee dust,
skipped through the day.
At night, they splashed clean

in a barrel of rainwater
before you wiped them
with hemmed feed sacks.

In summer, your hand prints
outlined the screen door,
after choring for neighbors.

Still warm, you raced home
with greens and butter beans,
"Mama, look what we got."

One night your brother
ran away, after a stropping
by your step-father.

Holding your mother's hand,
you were dragged down the steps
as she ran, looking. He was gone.

The next day she lay in bed.
One peek, and you dashed
to the toilet, then into

the kitchen, hurting.
You dragged a chair across
the floor to reach the skillet,

and prepared a tray
with salt pork and eggs.
You lifted each bite into her.

Many nights you slept at her feet,
while she sewed for others,
waking when the rocker stopped.

II

At sales, she lugged bolts
of material outside to check
their color. Then bargained.

With her homemade patterns,
cuts of cloth fit together,
held by sturdy seams.

One day at school, some boys
wiggled their hips, sneering,
"Jimmy ain't no himmy—he sews!"

Almost knowing what they meant,
a few laughed, and you ran
as that feeling of awfulness came,

the dizziness and gut pain.
You peed in your pants,
and kept running.

Missing school helped,
until your mother heard.
"Go speak to your father," she said,

and took you to the cemetery,
where you cried,
and were comforted.

For months after,
you carried an acorn
found on his grave,

then buried it when you learned
to scoop up courage
with a baseball and glove.

"Forgive all enemies,"
your mother said. You hated,
and hoped God understood.

III

A faded picture in a carriage,
a top hat, grey with mildew,
a medical degree from Knoxville

with its swirl of letters.
Bits of your father lived,
in the attic.

You always touched his name
three times, and spat.
Each day you dressed early,

that summer after high school,
taking odd jobs to pay for college.
Once, you wakened sucking your thumb.

Suddenly, you tasted
the bitterness of iodine
as you recalled Grandma Henry

dipping your right hand
into a smelly cup,
trying to cure your weakness.

One July afternoon, you buttoned
on a starched shirt, soon limp
with sweat, and hurried down

the road, through Miss Hattie's yard,
up Main, to Herb Jessep's bank.
Your bladder filled, as he stared.

He smoked a Cuban cigar, and crumpled
its wrapper over and over with his fingers.
"Can't do it, Jimmy," he said.

Trembling, you left with your hands
jammed in your pockets. That day, you smoked
the first of a lifetime of cigars.

By fall, your mother saved ten dollars,
and, with seven of your own, you entered
McTyeire College. There, home was a room

with a kitchen, over a hardware store.
You swapped lunches for cookware
with the owner. It was like trading

for bolts of cloth in Curve.
On campus, you hustled food,
the menu always the same—

beef sandwiches, potatoes
with a bacon-tomato sauce,
and tamales rolled in shucks,

kept hot in old newspapers.
Sitting cross-legged on a table,
you tailored in a men's store

two afternoons a week.
You kept the spools of thread,
the needles, the chalk,

the sewing machine and iron,
all close by, with shears
in a tin can, for safety.

You learned about the drape
of a pant, or the look of a crotch.
And you learned about the vanity of men.

On payday, you counted each penny,
and tore one corner off every
two dollar bill you touched.

IV

It was not going well.
Often, you gagged in class,
knowing you were not prepared.

After praying with your mother,
you accepted a traveling job,
and left college in mid-year.

With samples in the car,
you whizzed through Tennessee,
Mississippi, and Alabama.

When you were a boy,
those Tennessee towns
made your mouth dry,

and your hands damp.
Now, they were your territory.
Paris, Martin, Union City,

Dyersburg, and Curve—
where you often stopped, at noon,
and sat close to your father's grave.

You ate rat cheese on crackers,
and touched his headstone, as you left.
You spat three times.

On to Ripley, Covington,
and your new home, Memphis.
After two years of dating,

Jean Harris became your wife,
and partner on the road.
The first rift occurred

early in the marriage.
Jean surprised you
with champagne for dinner.

"Hard pennies beget soft dollars,"
you said, and carried the bottle
back to the store. Jean cried.

At night, you rented rooms
with kitchen privileges,
both of you tied in aprons.

You danced across southern ballrooms,
two-stepping to live bands.
"The Saint Louis Blues"

wailed from Beale Street
to the Peabody Hotel,
and pianos cut from

"You Didn't Believe Me"
to jazz guys playing ragtime.
You left the Peabody,

arm in arm,
leaving a meager tip
with a flourish.

While driving you ate peanuts,
and drank beer on hot days,
always looking for rest rooms.

To ease the long hours,
one of you started a song,
"I'll take you home again, Kathleen."

Jean carried the alto.
When tired, she lay on your shoulder,
with your hand between her legs.

Then the two daughters came,
and you loved them and her
on weekends. On Mondays

your eyes reddened while waving.
Alone. The dizziness. The road
was a rope, tightening. Sing.

"Brighten the corner where you are. . . ."

You picked up hitchhikers,
but talk was not enough.
That's how it started.

The women. The drinking.

Some weekends you didn't come home.
They were worse when you did.
Mother left you after nine years.

V

By 1928, you walked
on the red clay of Alabama,
and into a second marriage

with Anne Durham. She was
a teacher, a virgin, and
she called you "Arnold."

Home was Birmingham,
a city spawned by capitalists
from Montgomery, in search of iron.

They drilled through shale and sandstone,
dug for hematite, limestone, and coal,
and opened a blast furnace in 1880.

They named her Alice #1.
In a decade, Birmingham expanded
into "the Magic City."

Cross-state you traveled the old trails
of Chicasaws, Choctaws, Cherokees, Creeks.
Past their rivers. The Black Warrior, Tombigbee,

Alabama, Tallapoosa, and Coosa,
to the Cahaba, more central,
carrying its history to Birmingham.

The city ruptured into Jones Valley,
its perimeter the ore loins of Red Mountain
rising in semitropical sun and rain.

You, who did not know one bark from another,
bragged about Alabama trees.
The pines, loblolly and long leaf,

hemlock, haws, sweetgum, oak,
catalpa, pawpaw, sassafras, beech,
hornbeam, hackberry, ironwood, ash.

You included them all in a sweep
of the arm, nameless.
You boasted about Alabama plants and birds.

Azaleas, inkberry, wild olive,
goldenrod, sweet william, camellias,
yellowhammers and quail.

You, who never planted a flower,
you, who knew one bird from another
only if cooked and on the table.

Your delight about Alabama drew smiles
where there had been none. People remembered,
and that sold men's clothes.

After the great depression in 1893,
your mother often counted the coins
she earned sewing. She made little stacks

on top of her dresser, each stack
a payment for something. You listened
to the clinks over and over at night,

and years later wakened, scared.
Those clinks followed you everywhere,
and you worked hard to quiet them.

The first clothing store you owned,
on Fourth and Nineteenth,
was off the main pull.

Your hand stretched out to everybody

who came through the door
and on slow days
you stood on the sidewalk

introducing yourself.
"I'm Jimmy Arnold,"
and you talked them inside.

As long as one person wanted to buy, you stayed.

Some nights, going home over Shades Mountain,
you looked down on the city
into the fire-belches of the blast furnace

so like the explosions of war,
so unlike the explosions of war
in their restraint.

The surprise of each blast hit your stomach.
You teared at the yawn of lighted sky,
feeling as though through space

you looked into all of life,
the illusion soon gone as the molten iron ran
and finally darkened.

VI

You had one male friend, and one idol.
The friend, Clarence Kester, introduced you
to Roy B. Sewell, the idol.

As salesmen, you and Clarence split costs,
flipped a coin to make decisions,
and whistled at a lot of women.

When broke, you slipped out of hotels
on fire escapes, and laughed in your beer.
He stood with you at both weddings,

bringing his own second wife,
who got drunk and vomited
on Anne's linen tablecloth.

The night before the ceremony

the two of you drove to the Molton lobby.
Clarence dialed Jean's number in Memphis,
and held the receiver to your ear.

"Please come back, and bring our girls."
Your tongue felt swollen.
"I can't, Jimmy," she said.

And you wept in Clarence's arms,
unaware of the operator's voice in the phone,
not seeing the curious glances of people.

Two years later, Clarence called you about
the Sewells, Warren P., Robert A., and Roy B.
They were staking him, big.

Their plant made hundreds of suits,
and they needed lots of doors
with good salesmen inside.

That's how you got the first
Arnold Clothing Company.
One afternoon Clarence phoned.

"I have throat cancer. I need surgery."
You and Anne went to Atlanta that night.
After that, he spoke in a hoarse whisper.

After that, you saw a doctor twice a year,
and you peered into your mouth each morning,
while feeling lymph nodes in your neck.

VII

No one ignored Roy B. Sewell.
The youngest of the brothers,
he whirled into Birmingham

to check inventories and profit.
He appeared cordial, his Georgia accent,
like catfish and black-eyed peas,

catching you off-guard.
Sometimes a rod of steel surfaced,
its cold, unbending shape

pushing, when pushing was needed.
He wore one ring, a four carat diamond,
that was as well known as his parties.

Several suites were reserved at the Tutwiler,
and for two or three days, at all hours,
waiters, like jacketed highways,

ran between kitchen, bar, and someone playing
stride piano. The numbers of people grew,
little clusters, and one on one

all getting refills without asking.
Not many wives came. At other times,
Roy B. chose a few salesmen

to lunch with him at the Molton,
each of you accepting, quickly.
You were invited for thirty years.

Roy B. chose the waitress for those events.
She was young, a beginner, eager, hard-up.
He slipped a hundred dollar bill into her hand,

and watched her face as she counted the zeros.
You identified with both of them,
and heard the clinks from Curve.

VIII

Robert A. Sewell was not dapper.
He looked surprised, with raised eyebrows,
his graying hair combed oddly because of cowlicks.

His long arms and legs poked out of clothes
like hostages fighting for freedom,
unsure where they are going.

For years, he and Warren P. were salesmen.
They talked about clothes like some men talked
about women, each sale a conquest.

Robert A. was the Sewell who chose you.
"Jimmy, you belong with us," he said.
You almost saw him in a top hat and carriage.

Ten years later he was drowned in the tub,
a suicide. A penciled note floated limply.
He had kept his darkness inside.

The shock did not leave you.
At night you reached, crying, for Anne,
forgetting the twin beds that kept you uncoupled.

After that, you never bathed in a tub.
After that, you never drove to Curve alone,
and you subscribed to "A Prayer for the Day."

IX

Boots and Jean were your two daughters.
A premature baby, Boots was a screamer,
and easily startled. From the beginning

she and her step-father clashed.
He was forty and unused to children.
She was twelve and headstrong.

At fourteen, she boarded the L&N for Birmingham
while she and her mother sobbed, the depot at dawn
as alien as their bruised feelings.

Anne enrolled her in the Misses Howard's school,
for girls. They ate chicken salad at Loveman's,
and shopped for size three shoes.

A closeness came that often locked you out.
You scowled at expense, and the uncomfortable role
of day to day father. You forbade lipstick

before age sixteen, until Boots had her friends
lobby for her at a school party. You gave in,
not sure what it was all about.

After one year at the University of Alabama,
she eloped with a short redhead
who had a master's degree in metalurgy.

They ended up in California with two children,
their marriage often frantic and raw.
The mountains were to her a Chinese wall, and strange.

During episodes of depression, she called.
While talking to her, your voice faded,
and you handed the phone to Anne.

You were eighty-one when she died of cancer
after three wasting years. You sat,
half-slumped in the chair, repeating,

"Bye, baby girl. Bye."
And you lit a cigar with trembling fingers.
They scattered her ashes over the Sierras.

X

My early childhood is lost in ether
and metal hospital beds with high sides,
locked to keep me safe.

Only once did you dress in sterile whites,
paling, as you stood near the operating table,
Mother already holding my hand before surgery.

When the scalpel cut into my leg
you screamed, "Don't hurt her,"
and they carried you out, unconscious.

For a decade you paid those who saved my life.
On my seventh birthday, you mailed a letter, late,
with two checks—one for the hospital, one for me.

You wrote, "Your little presence is in my heart. . . ."
I kept the letter with a picture of you and Clarence
holding a child, her legs warmly wrapped.

One summer, while visiting Birmingham,
I readied the store with you in the mornings.
You sprinkled sawdust on the oiled wood floor,

handed me a wide black broom,
and I swept out the day-before,
onto the sidewalk, into the street.

You straightened stacks of pants,
picked cigar butts out of the toilet,
and opened rolls of coins for the cash box.

You never tired of this routine.
During my Birmingham-Southern years,
I lived with you and Anne,

but seldom came home before bedtime.
Sometimes, returning late after a concert,
the bus left me two miles from the house.

Each of you had a car, yours a cadillac.
I was not allowed to drive them
except to run an errand for you.

While reading the paper one night,
you learned I was an honor student.
"I wanted to finish college," you said.

When I talked about becoming a doctor,
you walked out of the room, gagging.
I heard the toilet flush.

You were not unkind, just adamant
that I could not stick it out.
Weeks later you dreamed

a ship loaded with green paper and medical supplies
sank from the weight of its cargo, the captain failing
to pull the ship into harbor with a threaded needle.

You waked, sweating, slept,
and dreamed again about a child
lost in an attic in Curve.

Halfway through the first year
at medical school, a belly pain
sent me to the emergency room.

The appendectomy took seventeen minutes,
but I missed ten days with my cadaver.
I returned from Tuscaloosa to talk about it.

You put your arm around my shoulders
as we walked down Twentieth Street.
"Never give up," you said. "You are a Arnold."

Over the years you bragged about Boots,
the homemaker, Jean, the doctor.
One day you said to me,

"Roy B. wanted his son to be a doctor,
but he couldn't make the grades."
And you smiled, taking a long drag on a fresh cigar.

XI

In 1938, you entered the race
for the governor of Alabama.
At age forty-six, you needed to reach.

In running for office, your pitch
was "pay as you go." You saved copies
of every newspaper that printed your name.

Customers began calling you "Governor,"
and when they promised you their vote,
a free tie went into their suit box.

Five men were candidates.
The favorite, by far,
was Frank M. Dixon,

a native Californian
with a cork leg,
who practiced law in Birmingham.

During the campaign, you became known
as a man who watched his pennies.
You hired a black quartet to sing

spirituals, and printed your name
in small letters beneath theirs,
at every rally. Then you charged

the public for entertainment.
After the election, you didn't owe a cent.
It was during this time you gave

a suit of clothes to each baseball player
who hit a home run for the Birmingham team.
Your name was heard more often than the coach's.

On January 17th, 1939 Frank M. Dixon took office.
The results were clear. You ran last with 1,201 votes.
Frank Dixon, the new governor, received 152,860.

That was the end of your political career.

XII

One Sunday, in 1928, you walked into a Presbyterian church
for a free chicken dinner, and met Anne Durham.
A graceful neck softened her sharp features.

She walked rapidly, as though ten minutes late,
and expecting a reprimand.
You were usually several steps behind.

At church, you became a couple,
and you felt the pull of settling down, again,
the relief of leaving the chase. You married.

She left you often, at first,
angry that you pushed her into deception.
Her secret lay-aways increased,

though you chided her about the money.
She resented your post-dated checks,
and your bartering. An overcoat paid

the dentist. Gasoline was a shirt and tie.
Fresh vegetables from a customer cost a hat.
And over the years, there were rumors about women.

The arguments pushed you behind newspapers,
and into lengthy days at the stores.
For years, other people kept you together.

You invited friends to your home,
and sought couples to share vacations.
Both of you reached out to Anne's family.

The Durham children worried about their father,
an unlicensed veterinarian who tromped with farmers
tending injured fetlocks, or hurrying to a cow

stalled in labor. His simple office was carpeted
with mud and wet barn smells. A drunk, he was
finally committed to a hospital in Tuscaloosa.

Anne did not want liquor in "her" home,
and when you broke the rule,
anger lasted for hours.

You won that struggle, and in later years
she drank port wine with you at dinner.
Sometimes, she got tipsy without knowing it.

During Christmas, you visited her brother and family.
He peddled his own recipe of "vim herb" into a million,
then invested in cattle and pepsi in Carolina.

You enjoyed the aura of a wealthy brother-in-law.
Anne's sister married a guitar player
who sang and talked on radio at six A.M.

He drawled, "Arnold Clothing Company,
the poor man's friend, when better clothes
are sold, Arnold will sell them."

You wakened everyone in the house to listen.
Gently, you leaned on all things
that would hold you.

For the usual reasons, there was no divorce,
but mainly, you did not want to relive
Curve again, and dusty roads,

and wanting to run to your father.
It was a tight gut torn by worry.
It was the door of a hotel opening into nothing.

In your late seventies, you still drove to work
each day, with Anne. She did more and more,
at times, her energy carrying both of you.

She laid out your clothes, helped you bathe,
combed your hair and brows. Even zipped your pants.
As always, she corrected your English.

Years before, you sold all but this store.
Your savings kept it open, now.
Roy B. told you it was a bad decision,

but you could not let go.
Daily, you walked into the bank next door,
shaking hands, smiling at the teller girls

who offered you coffee and cheese crackers.
"Here's our Mr. Jim," they'd say.
You ate slowly, and added water to the coffee.

Anne worked in the store with you,
rushing from bookkeeping to alterations,
tending to details you no longer saw.

Those around you worried.
What would you do without her?
"I'll never leave my home," you said.

Within months after your death,
Anne moved into a small apartment.
She began to withdraw, even from church.

She stopped driving, and depended on friends
to take her shopping, or to circle the mountain
for lunch at Morrison's.

Five years later, after moving into a cousin's home,
she wakened at six, and walked two miles with a neighbor.
She took several short trips, and wrote letters.

"I couldn't stop grieving for so long," she said.
The marriage had lasted forty-five years.
Some nights she may still drink a little port.

XIII

You stood on the sidewalk looking
at the clearance signs in your windows,
knowing the doors would be locked

after forty years. Walking inside,
you touched a smooth material, its texture
so different from the rough wools in Curve.

You glanced at the pile of flat boxes
with the large print, "Arnold Clothing Company."
A package of stale crackers lay nearby.

You stared at the floor-length mirrors,
saw your mother's lines, faint now,
giving way to the universal look of the old,

giving way to the blood vessels asking for rest.
In your reflection, you still looked for your father,
but the pictures of him never told you enough.

He always stayed so strong in you.
With labored breath you hummed, "I come to the garden—."
Three figures came through the door, toward you.

You smiled and stuck out your hand, "I'm Jimmy Arnold."
And then you saw them—
Stockings covered their faces.

Two hands grabbed and held you,
while someone yanked off your belt.
He hit you with the buckle, until you fell.

They stole eleven dollars from the cash box,
and ran,
and were never caught.

You never quite came back after that,
and you died that summer in July,
in your own bed, where you wanted to die.

Three

The Great Jazz Piano Celebration

I

Marian McPartland sat behind the long table
with George Shearing and an usher,
her English accenting each word.

The harsh hues of makeup
gave her a punk look
of sliding blue eyelids
and orange sag lines decades deep.

She smiled with every autograph,
and scribbled what the fan requested,
those fingers
still moving quickly,
after miles of travel on a Steinway.

II

People tried to avoid Shearing's blindness,
glancing away from his eyes
as though he could see them stare.

The usher guided his left hand
over a stained album,
writing in big script.
A young bearded man,
with manicured nails,
reached for the jacket,
heavy with seventy-eights,
and pushed close to the pianist,
telling him it was a great gig.

One woman, with long earrings,
snatched her purchase from the usher
and said, "Shit, I could have signed that myself."

It was close to midnight.

Sally

Little sound
gets into me.

I start the engine,
straining to hear,

never knowing for sure
if the motor's running.

I sometimes return,
smell the exhaust,

and see the keys
in the ignition.

The ringing static
inside my head

hurls noise against
the quiet outside.

On the highway I drive
slowly, wavering

as the suck of the semi
rocks my car.

The mirrored
lips of passers

curse. Some give me
the finger, and yell.

I want to ram them.
Above, nimbus clouds

alert me. Gusts
bully the road,

then shiver quiet
into the rain.

Silence. Drivers
in the slosh.

It is as close as
they come to knowing.

I wave as a car toots by,
and wave again

at a train panting
parallel to the road.

This Is the Gospel

I was told as a child
that Martha Van
ended up loony

after a black cat
crossed in front of her
on the County Fork road.

They said she didn't
turn her car around,
or count to nine.

The older kids swore
the cat was a witch
or Satan himself.

When they put Miss Van away,
she kept mumbling that
the world looked black,

and she believed her head
was burning in Hell's fire.
She dunked her hair in water.

Willie Bill said the fire
from the cat's fur
went straight to her brain.

Our preacher, Brother Sommers,
agreed with Willie. One Sunday
he told us about witches

voodooing cats into evil.
He said just about
everybody knew that.

Miss Van was supposed
to marry Neville Stone,
but he was drafted.

Mama said they were shy,
and kept to themselves.
I heard they read to each other.

After Neville was killed
by the Germans, people said
Miss Van almost died, too.

A package stamped "Fragile"
came from him the very day
she learned he died.

It was a set of china.
The next year she began teaching,
and sometimes invited people for tea.

She held her cup in both hands,
staring hard at something
nobody else could see.

Brother Sommers said she washed
each cup, every day,
whether used or not,

put them on the top shelf
of the china clost,
and turned the key.

One day in her class we talked
about John L. Lewis, and I said
his eyebrows looked like the tail

of a scared cat. Somebody laughed,
then meowed. That's how all the fuss
about black cats got started.

Miss Van said superstition
was plain ignorance, and
everybody ought to know that.

She said the English
kept black cats for luck,
but feared white cats.

Before she went crazy,
Willie Bill was traipsing
in and out with tools,

unplugging her sink,
when a throw rug
skidded. He smacked

into the china closet,
banging it hard
against the wall.

Miss Van didn't move.
Didn't shed a tear.
Just watched him sweep up.

Later, she drove into the country,
and that's when the black cat
ran in front of her.

Ward C

Under the October moon
we drive there.
The wild cells scattered,
and our friend is too still.
As her eyes get big,
we see less of her in them.

She felt the thing in her
after a month on the job,
and rushing her in pain
through the swinging doors,
we gave her to them.
The cutting out of it,
the radiation that beamed
its unseen heal, all came
so soon.

At work, again, she threw
her wig into the air, and let
us feel the fuzz on her scalp.
Hundreds of Jews passed before
me, shaved, starving, looking
through the barbed fences.

Her thinness grew, and we
all knew the bad about to
come. Next, to Mayo's.
They saw the worst,
and sewed her up
with a cannula in her gut.
An ambulance sirened
her here.

I always know where
the exits are in a hospital.
The toilets are close,
with stalls where I can go
to hide the trembling.
I count the number of steps
to the nearest elevator.

Across the hall,
a small, gowned man waits
for his food to be tabled.
A bowl of soup, and a cup,
steaming. All of him works
to breathe. He sips,
spilling the wet, unnoticed.

I look away. The room
is getting too warm.
In a low voice, I suggest
leaving. Our friend
may tire. As we turn
toward the door, I try
not to run.

The Beauty Shop

Mona squats on a stool,
her flat arches comforted
by a lower rung,

her trade zipped
in a nylon bag
that sits on the counter.

She calls this room "the kitchen."
The funeral home pays her double,
and the work takes only half the time.

The client's hair is already washed.
Mona wets it down with alcohol
instead of water,

and only the top and sides are set—
no one sees the back. Usually,
the corpse is one of her old customers.

Today, the woman under the sheet
has been positioned with her hands
crossed over her abdomen,

while her head is raised
and tipped slightly to the right.
Her upper and lower lids are closed

over plastic cusps inserted into her eyes.
The mouth is wired shut, with the excess wire
out of sight between the teeth.

Once, Mona was sneaked into "the kitchen"
to watch the pump and aspirator attack
the body like metal vampires,

but she ran out sick
when the gutters filled
with the stench of formaldehyde.

That same night, she and the mortician
drank a fifth of Nauvoo wine,
while she was waiting for a client to dry,

and, giggling, they ended up in a coffin
in the back room, naked. His wife came
downstairs, and turned on the light.

They heard her coming, and closed the lid.
The incident was never mentioned, but Mona
gets fewer calls, and misses the money.

Now, she finishes, quickly,
combs, fluffs, and sprays,
then hurries out the side door.

Overnight

It is hard to see
in the white-greys of shy light.

I pack the grips in my car
with less care than yesterday.

As the cooler drains
I make a last check

glancing at the unmade bed
with its twisted marriage

of sheet and blanket.
I have nothing to leave.

The doctor says I must
try this, alone, and see.

In the lobby, I take a receipt,
and pass a phone near the door.

The ignition is on. I can feel
the car move. When I adjust the mirror,

my motel, an outline in mist,
wavers like a First Grade drawing.

A Forerunner

Doubts came, soon
after I moved in
that night.
We asked too much
about the others.

Often, my lips tightened
when you walked in late,
and you swore it was He
ringing us after midnight.

Partial resolutions came,
awkwardly, leaving
tiny compartments
of isolation,
that hung there,
like curtains.

Then one noon,
you threw my bags
onto the bed,
and you tried,
only once, to stop me.

Restoration

Let me lie down beside you
to rest,
away from easy sex,
and the synthetic heads
of drums.

Let me count the violets
as we sit,
and see their purple
against the sky,

still fresh. Each leaf
has a life to give
for the asking.

I am asking.

This quiet with you
will go,
but the purple
is so sweet.

The Taker

She was very slight,
with skin almost pale, it was so fair.
Dressed in bright plaid, her mind,
behind dark eyes, seemed in charge
as she shopped in the store
asking about a Monet or some little

trinket. Then, to sweaters, with little
scarfs nearby. There was a slight
stop as she felt one, while the store
clerks talked among themselves, a fair
number of them openly bored. She had a charge
account here. Her husband spoke his mind

about it. When her bills came, he reminded
her he saw the balance, no matter how little
it was. Often, at bedtime, he charged
into their room, accusing her of slighting
him. During breakfast, he spoke of being fair
to him when asking for money, then began his store

of endless criticism. Often, she left to store
things in the pantry, trying to keep her mind
occupied. She listened, knowing about his affairs
in and out of the office. A friend sent the little
rumors running home. She knew why he made slight
excuses for being late. She wanted to charge

into him, kicking, hitting. Instead, her charge
was against a revolving door, into one store
of pretties, then another, sometimes slighting
people who spoke. So tense, now, her mind
felt swollen, and each item seemed too little
to pick up, quickly. The October day, fair

until now, was lost in light rain, with a fairly
big crowd trapped inside, waiting to charge
into the wet, shivering. She paused, hid a little
camera in her bag, and began walking out the store.
Without turning her head, she looked, her mind
full of every detail seen, even slight

movement. She fairly flitted through the store,
feeling good, in charge. A man was coming. Her mind
had little time to act. He came, his touch slight.

Little Thing

he lay there without life
part of the road

rubbered to death
his warm breath gone

taken by a blow
so quick and harsh

no thump was felt
by one moving on

At the Hampton

By morning everybody knew
about Jamie. His old
jumping rope with the wood handles
had been long enough for the hanging.
They all knew his story about the rope,
and how at forty he began training
for old age. But after he stiffened,
the rope was curled around a football,
and thrown in the bottom of his trunk.
In 1935, he won the trunk in a raffle
at the fraternity house, and on top,
in big letters, he stamped
"The Crimson Tide."

He had talked a lot about dignity.
In the war he fought "with dignity,"
he married a woman with it,
he operated a shoe store with it.
And he buried his wife and one son
with it, after a plane crash.

Bloated from the rope, he lay now,
strapped on a gurney that took him.
From his room, there were faint shouts.
Two men in wheel chairs, and another
leaning on a walker. They were circled
around his trunk, laughing, celebrating
Jamie. He'd done it. With a rope
he'd used when his legs could bend.
They gave a yell for "The Crimson Tide,"
then, with dignity, left his room.

Let's Play Cowboy

The cowboy drank his whiskey
straight. No chaser.
Burning the dust and dung
from his throat.

The cowboy drank
in tonky saloons,
doing in the bad guys,
saving the town and his lady.

When I was eight,
my whiskey was water.
I gulped it,
and practiced gunning
by repeated draws
from a child's holster.

Sometimes I went to war.
I rode with Lee
against the yankees,
never stopping at Appomattox.

On Saturdays, I snacked
through the double feature,
and saw the same town
filmed all over the west.
Wagon wheels rotated backwards.

Now my guns are gone, strapped
to the broomhandle bays
that have splintered away
with Hopalong Cassidy.

The guns are gone. Left in
London and Dunkirk and Guam.
Left in Korea and Nam. Guys,
good and bad, left.

Now, at the Bijou, the old films
keep the cowboys young, as they
dismount. Their celluloid eyes
stare before the quick draw.
The rusty bullets don't wait.
How to play? Cowboy, I drink.

The Garbage Storm

Earlier, I heard the wind.
A smash of metal
against the garage
echoed into a downpour.
Lightning directed
the thunder bursts
so close I wished
for the old storm cellar,
its heavy wooden
doors closed over us.

From every drive,
tumbling acts of swill
blasted into trees,
shingles, and screens.
Bloated papers coated
wires as cardboard boxes
banged into the fence.
Something broke a pane
in my gas lamp, and I saw
the flame falter.

I walked down the road
looking for my green
cans and tops. They were
scattered blocks away,
but I picked them up,
knowing them from
all the other green.

One top had a streak
of teak stain on it,
the other, two holes
punched all the way
by a carpenter's nail.
One bottom had a crooked
plastic screw holding
its handle, the second
had spots of tar inside.
These were mine.

I pushed both tops
into one can, then dumped
one can into the other,
and dragged them home.

The Magazine

Two doors open a small lounge
into the big room of bodies
in the DeGowin Blood Center.

A woman, sagging on blue-covered chrome,
flips through a tumble of magazines,
and settles into a fingered ATLANTIC
(printed in big red) December, 1983.

Only her eyes move.
She suckles a low moan—
Jane was with me
the day the rain dropped a squirrel like that.

She sees their cairn
in the rearview mirror,
splashing hard,

hears little Bill
bang against the door,
sees it open,
her hand grabbing for air.

"It's Strutsy, Mama!"
his voice gone,
swallowed in thunder.

The flat whack of the body.
He lay in the street breathing and bleeding—
the driver behind her hits the rain,
not seeing Bill in it.

a time of near-death,
we have come to know its length and its look—
She is called into the big room,

into the hustle,
into the chair, and tilted back.
After the rain, the trees were prettier yet.
The needle goes into her.

They know her story.
They know Bill is upstairs,
a mask strapped over his nose and mouth,
("I'm Halloween, Mama!")
while his bulging belly is filled
with the mushed sounds of gloved hands.

They know she must give
of herself, while she waits.
It is not a new story, but they listen.
Someone takes THE ATLANTIC from her,

and asks if she likes the magazine.
She nods, and does not speak.
She sees Bill climbing high into a tree.

Four

A Sun of Fireflies

Why wait any longer?
Catch a wave as a plaything,
and balance an exploding star

until tomorrow.
Don't count the ragged pulse
that tunes the fickle beat.

Let the oboe sound its A,
and hear the music rise
to a hollow tree,

where the reedy sound
of a barred owl
coaxes in the night.

Go above the cities to the
sky bursts, unabridged in time.
The mottled blue

shapes into marbles
we dare to hold.
Why wait longer?

Muse

the first trumpet muted
into the verse,
and the concert was right
in sound

like your hand on mine
tapping
unsung tunes with rhythm

but an end came,
and I bodied out of the hall,
lost in images
that sent me somewhere

away

with feelings so big
they scared me

unlike steel doors
locked the third west
or tachycardia at three A.M.

The Barn Swallows

They must, is why. And the same
for me, waiting the winter in the
gray, till May. Winging fast,
they land, paired, on last year's
grass and mud. Wit-wit.

In swallow-tail coats, back
from Córdoba or La Paz, catching
mosquitoes and flies by the Amazon,
into Caracas, filling their bellies
for flight. Asleep at night.

To my light, on the garage,
and I tape the switch still,
its heat one less predator.
The incoming wires their floor
on which to preen. I peer through
the screen, see them drawn
against the cauliflower clouds
in the ravine. Wit-wit.

The eggs come. The sitting
parent pants in the sun.
Each fifteen minutes, first one,
then its mate, flutters in and out,
the off-nest swallow darting
low toward the river.

For miles they fly, chasing
cold-blooded bits of prey.
Their young wait. Four beaks
on black fuzz, looking
like minstrel men. At dusk
a cat stalks my yard. I yell.

He comes, again and again, and
he comes with the night while I sleep.
My eyes open at unheard sounds.
I look this dawn, gone, the nest,
mauled, below. A few feathers
lie small in the dew.

Days go. Suddenly, a pair is there,
wit-witting in circles, and mud
is in their beaks. Grass is tucked
into the sides. It is growing,
five inches of rounded home, ready
for its clutch. There is the steady
come and go. The cracking of birth,

and a dearth of room. Fledgling rears
hang over the edge, plopping white
waste to the ground. One by one
they wing to the wire, flailing
like kites that need more tail.

For days, the swallows return,
in twos or fours or sixes,
flying in circles as they twit.
Never landing. They flock
in the cold wind.

They must, is why. I am drawn,
thinking of the tides I have run
bared, splashing. Having gone
the roads I know their hollow stare.
So staying, I watch the undyed quilt
of snow shrink in the longer days,
then rub my face in the early thaw
to wake my wintered skin.

The Cutting

After they did the cutting,
those few trees changed.
All limbs near the road
are hacked away,
leaving the back boughs
guarded by pine needles.

The fresh wounds tarred
darker than the bark
cast a stippled look,
as though a storm
is blowing in, slashing
the sea high on a coastline.

While stumbling over cones
on my own butchered limb,
I saw the huddled clouds
in southern woods.
I bared my legs
on heavy sand,

tanning all but the scars
that stayed white. The deep
cuts filled, if I watered
them, and I could float a
paper boat down my thigh.

Down the road, I limp
to the crippled trees,
and watch the green
inhale the sun.
The stubs loom, clearly.

Flapping, one into the other,
the back boughs fan
the stricken trunk.
Never sure, their needles
tremble in the air.
Cars pass. Minutes.

The sticky smell
hangs. Waiting.
There it is.
The metal pitch
of a gutting saw.
But it's faint,
in the far away,
down another road.

The Road Worker

It is the fourth week
of this. The elms
did not fight the big
machines. The sudden
wideness seems far
from home. I could
be on any road.

A worker crawls
on the asphalt,
behind the steam
of fresh black.
He drags a coil
of hemp. One thin
line of string lies

for miles, limply
centered, waiting
for yellow spray.
Last night he stowed
the coil in front
of the seventh
baluster of the bridge,

off for the weekend.
It stays, an odd heap.
I make extra trips,
just to see. Doesn't
he know? Someone will
steal it or dangle
it in the river.

It's Monday, and I near
the bridge, early, with
the swallows. The hemp
is gone, leaving a clean
circle. Then I see his kneeling body at work,
an easy mark, as we pass.

The Death of the Trees

Like bewildered soldiers, they stand,
still surprised that death came
from backwater, staying.

The Planners

I think wild,
trying to find a way in.
As in all jungles, some of us
circle wide and sniff.

For months, hard hat areas
fenced in my daily trails
and watering sites.

Stampeding streets
were cut off like cattle,
damned with walks of uneven
Purington paver bricks.

Workers gutted strong maples and ashes,
and later planted maples and ashes,
and petunias near andorras
within walls of railroad ties.

They added wood benches
with bi-polar legs sunk in dirt,
and a fountain

of water slitting
out of iron pipes,
with one small stream spurting
through the concrete base

like the blowhole in a tooth whale—
all of it splashing onto
Purington paver bricks.

To link street levels,
they built three long steps
with railroad ties for risers,

then added zig-zagging banister
that, like mirrors in a "crazy house,"
make walking an olympic event.

There is a happy-red popcorn wagon
with yellow wheels,
parked below the first step
farther down the mall,

its color and smell
pulling me into the tent at Baraboo.
The only handrail stands hidden
by the white puffs of food.

Away from the plaza, cars are housed
in huge cement hulks that muscle upward,
the flow of traffic controlled
by electronic arms that demand cash.

The top of the ramp feels
like a San Francisco hill
with none of its beauty,
and when circling down,
brakes are pumped all the way.

A change will come
as the talling shadows of maples
spread their age over the
railroad ties. And farmers,

who once spat from the bank steps
on Saturday night, will see
their sallow stains flushed away
by one small stream spurting
above the bricks.

The Wood Steps Revisited

I climb to here in silence.
Old train whistles, that blew like pan flutes
through the journey, thin into tunes I know.
Puffy eyed and stiff, I dance the jig.

Stair-Glide

The seat snugs into the tracks,
stilled until I ride it.
Reels and cams distort
my stairway into unknowns
that are just words to me.

I want to do it while I am alone
in the house. With just the dogs.
How did the pitch get so steep?
Like that sloping trail in Bandera
when my horse stumbled halfway down.

I mount side-saddle, sliding
both feet onto the footrest.
Only thirteen steps. I spit
three times between my fingers,
then push. The Lamborghini soars.

Etching

we have looked at the world
over years of loving
when you have shown me
half a cheek

uncovered, fresh with morning,
branded with the weight
of your head upon a pillow
or a rumpled spot of rest

your face lines
have taken root,
and spread
like maples,

leaving
the light strokes
of birch to grow
around your eyes

In Two Dimensions

I don't know when the world map
was pasted there. Much of the tape
is curling back onto itself, letting go.
Every day, it is with me while I type.
Seas frisk on printed shores
renewing me with cold spray.
I follow a gull upward,

and lose it in the earth's
yearly sundance.
Warming its blue robe,
the pirouetting ball tilts
around the fire, one speck
in a putting together of millions.

I feel the sweat of God
in Genesis, and remember
a thumbed copy of that
beginning open in church
with a torn bit of paper clipped
to it saying, "This is the answer."

That which goes or stays is happening,
and I am in it. My fingers, less agile,
peck for words as a gull glides high.
No rock dove claps its wings, guided
to the home loft with answers.

If the map falls,
and the oceans splash
one into the other,
I will need time to dry.
Then I will walk on every beach
and wait for a single tide.

The I of Me Now

It is time, A.M. time,
with a passing fog of cars
smoking by. Away from most
others, I live unevenly,
in hours shaped by whim.
I see kids rush, chewing
as they go, swallowing whole
the bulk of day. Talling up
over the winter's passing,
they dream of the hoops
of spring when they pass,
from hand to net, the
quick shot of success.

Looking through the slingshots
of snow-rigged trees, I am a face
in the chimney of winter.
In a sketch of many rectangles,
I will get smaller as the
distance grows, but today
I watch a lumbersome bug
climb a bedroom wall.
I talk with students
flinging their lives
into the bursts
of headlines.

In the car, I drive with jeans
unzipped, letting the sag of comfort
ride with me. I take an extra
caramel, and feel the sweet saliva
wash my mouth. I wiggle to
syncopation, and toss myself
into Brazil with a basa nova.
I play the swollen chords of Mahler.

The time? It is A.M., again,
and my face will find a window.
Only the dilated eyes of night
look in, and that is hours away.